Esquire's

Easy business etiquette for complicated times

THINGS A MAN SHOULD KNOW ABOUT. . .
Handshakes,
White Lies,
and Which Fork Goes Where

Ted Allen and Scott Omelianuk

Library of Congress Cataloging-in-Publication Data
Allen, Ted.
    Esquire things a man should know about handshakes, white lies, and which fork goes
    where: easy business etiquette for complicated times / by Ted Allen and Scott Omelianuk.
       p. cm.
    ISBN 1-58816-068-8
    1. Business etiquette—Humor. 2. Etiquette for men—Humor. 3. Etiquette—Humor.
    I. Omelianuk, Scott. II. Title.

    HF5389.A43 2001
    395.5'2'0207—dc21

                      2001024796

DESIGN BY SERG ANDREYEV, NEUWIRTH & ASSOCIATES, INC.
COVER DESIGN BY TODD ALBERTSON
COVER ILLUSTRATIONS © 2001 CSA IMAGES

First Edition
1 2 3 4 5 6 7 8 9 10

Printed in Mexico
www.esquire.com

Contents

introduction 1

It all begins with the handshake—and thus so shall we.

one 4

First off, here we have some special body language that tells people you have no plans to kill them.

two 14

Shine the wing tips. Dust off the Louis Vuitton. It's the 10 A.M. job interview.

three 24

What are my strengths and weaknesses? Well, for starters, I have a weakness for authority figures who hold my destiny in the oily palms of their dirty little hands.

four 32

We've got your workday casual—right here: Clothes do, it turns out, make the man.

five 40

The Long March, aka Bataan via Camry, aka the commute.

six 44

Life in the cubicle (and the hallway and the break room and the supply closet).

seven 56

I'm mad as hell, and I'm going to salve my rage in a soothing chat with one of several thousand disinterested phone reps—yeah, that's the ticket.

eight 70

This liverwurst sandwich property of Lucine Kasbarian—do not touch!!!

nine 78

It's 11:37 and we're damned pleased to meet you.

ten 90

Your gal Friday, who, chances are better than fifty-fifty, might prefer not to be called a "gal."

eleven 108

The three-Pellegrino lunch.

twelve 130

The two o'clock meeting (ha—made you yawn).

thirteen 140

Courtesies and niceties inside and outside the office, including door holding and what to do about people who don't smell right.

fourteen 154

I did not have relations with that woman.

fifteen 168

The four P.M. sales call, wherein Mr. Jones wishes you to contemplate the merits of his company's very special manila clasp envelopes.

sixteen 174

Afternoon delight: sex in the workplace.

seventeen 186

You don't bring me flowers, although you now and again come through with a Maglite.

eighteen 190

On firing the scalawag you just caught having afternoon delight. On your desk. Plus: dignity when it's your own head on the veritable chopping block.

Introduction

It all begins with the handshake—and thus so shall we.

It launches every great partnership, every brilliant deal, every campaign and treaty and used-car sale. It is the first thing we must do as we stride into each new corner of the world—that is, to make an impression on its occupants—and pressing the flesh is among our first such opportunities.

One such impression might be that you sweat no more than the next guy. Another, so long as there are no weapons in your paw, is that you have no plans to kill anybody just this minute—people never get tired of that. Also favorably regarded is your disinclination to serve as a vector for dysentery, thus, the custom of extending the *right* hand for greeting purposes, reserving the left for germy personal cleansing. It is ironic in these fussy, antibacterial times that some men prefer to shake no hands at all, not even the right one. Among the more famously fastidious is onetime presidential hopeful Donald Trump, who called the custom "barbaric."

Well, it is not barbaric. (Trump, on the other hand...) Quite the opposite, in fact. It is the quintessential gesture of masculine civility. And it has persisted, like most time-honored rituals of etiquette and courtesy, arbitrary or odd or archaic though they may seem, because it works.

Etiquette, you could argue, has gotten a bad rap among the putatively rougher sex. The word evokes society mavens, heiresses to breakfast-cereal fortunes, prissy people and their effete, fey, girly functions, mostly weddings and debutante balls. Not so. So very, very not so. No aspect of human endeavor has more byzantine codes of conduct than the business world, and nowhere are the stakes as high—we're not talking here about being dropped from the social register when you make a mistake; we're talking about your no longer being able to afford food. The rituals and conventions of business, they help us project an image of ourselves as smart, traveled, sophisticated, and self-assured. They help everyone know where they stand in your eyes and where you stand in theirs. They allow us to convey to our fellow travelers such things as regard, respect, and friendliness, a sense of prospective sharedness-of-purpose. The handshake, well tendered, it says: You are a pro. I am a pro. We are smart and prepared and not to be trifled with—and now, let us conduct some commerce.

What is perhaps more important: Not only do rules of conduct apply to you, they are your *friend*. Your very good friend. When you know the rules—what not to order at a lunch meeting, how to fire somebody, how to ask for a raise, when to kiss a client (not often)—your knowledge does more than just make you look good to other people. It makes you feel relaxed and comfortable. It becomes second nature, an integral part of your personal style. And that looking good to other people, that comfort in even uncomfortable situations, well, when you've got the same seniority as the other guys, it's *the* thing that helps you get ahead.

Or to put it another way, it helps you attain what Esquire has always helped men attain—that sophistication and confidence that we like to call Man at His Best.

So let us go forth, then, freshly steeled in the face of danger, strong before difficulties, and let us wheel and deal and shape new worlds. Let's sign on the dotted line, and mean it. And just as it all begins, so must it conclude—let us shake on it.

Pleasure doing business with you.

Chapter one

First off, here we have some special body language that tells people you have no plans to kill them

Seeing as how all business starts with the handshake, let us as well: The handshake shall be firm, fast, and free of excess perspiration.

Translation: *Firm* means a squeeze, but not a hard squeeze.

Fast means that this squeeze happens in an instant and is not sustained.

As for perspiration, that was discreetly wiped off on your trousers a few seconds ago.

The practice of handshaking arose in part as a good-faith gesture that one's right paw contained no weaponry.

Also, in some cultures, handshaking is reserved for the right hand, whereas, for excellent and hygienic reasons, the most personal of personal cleansing tasks is reserved for the left.

Something to keep in mind when considering the previous note: Not everybody is right-handed—but we digress.

The best handshake: two firm, quick, and confident pumps, followed by release.

People in other cultures shake hands differently.

Businesspersons in some African countries, for example, tend to retain their grip much longer than businesspersons in the U.S.

Policy for shaking hands with people in other cultures: When in Rome. . .

It's called respect.

Respect for other people, you see (and their prospectively proportional regard for you), is the guiding principle behind all matters of etiquette.

Also: When you know how to behave, you are comfortable, you are relaxed, you are at your best.

Not *that* relaxed: Augmenting the handshake with a brief thumb-wrestle, the knocking of fists atop one another, the "giving" of "five," or any similar flourish is acceptable in a business context only for boxers, fraternity brothers, and members of boy bands.

Extending one's hand as if to shake, then suddenly withdrawing same and smoothing back one's hair: You, Fonzie, are fired.

It is sometimes useful to lend a moderate extra measure of affection to a handshake by bringing up the left hand and patting the shoulder.

Engulfing your colleague's hand with both of yours: if you are a Protestant minister or consoling the widow at a funeral or, of course, Bill Clinton.

The handshake that starts as a handshake but is then used to pull you into a hug: You must decide whether to submit to such affection on a case-by-case basis.

It's usually easiest to just give in and let yourself be hugged.

Afterward, you can cease all future business activities with promiscuous huggers, unless your business is the recording of hip-hop music.

Or unless you come to realize that you really needed a hug, which you probably did.

When to shake a woman's hand (old school): when she extends hers first.

When to shake a woman's hand (modern view): whenever you would shake any businessperson's hand.

When to kiss the cheek of a businessperson who happens to be a woman: when, and only when, the woman is your wife, your mother, or your daughter, and there better be no tongue with those last two.

Additional time to kiss a businesswoman's cheek: when she has inexorably begun the process of kissing yours.

Warning: Do not pretend to miss her cheek and "accidentally" kiss her mouth.

Believe it or not, there are still some people who actually attempt this pathetic move—although they're not likely to remain employed for long.

When to kiss a businessperson's *hand*: when he is the pope.

Some people, notably people from southern California, believe it acceptable to refuse to shake hands with someone known to have a cold. These people are wrong.

What you do rather than refuse to shake hands: You go ahead and shake hands, and then, shortly thereafter, you excuse yourself and wash yours.

Refusing to shake a proffered hand is deeply insulting and appropriate only where said hand belongs to the most odious of human creatures—we're talking KKK Imperial Wizard territory here.

When you have a cold: Tell people you're not shaking hands today because you have a cold; they will thank you, and, who knows, the practice may eventually become commonplace.

Yup, respect.

Now then: Imagine that it is 8:00 A.M., and that opportunity spreads limitless before you. Let us, friend, seize the proverbial day.

As soon as we vow never again to say, "seize the day."

Chapter two

Shine the wing tips. Dust off the Louis Vuitton. It's the 10:00 A.M. job interview

Perhaps we have gotten ahead of ourselves, because before one can behave appropriately on the job, one must become employed.

When writing to request employment: Address your letter not Dear Sir or Dear Madam or Personnel, but to the actual person in charge.

Regarding that person in charge: You check company literature or the firm's Web site or call an assistant in her company to verify that you've got her name and title and address absolutely correct.

And then you put into practice these two words: spell check.

When writing to request employment: personal stationery, not the letterhead of a current or previous employer.

Especially if your current employer is Fatburger.

Your personal stationery shall be plain in aspect and lacking in such decoration as balloons and clowns.

Your résumé: laser-printed on high-quality white or off-white paper.

Qualities that this résumé paper should lack: glitter, marbling, metallic flecks, plasticity.

Do not lie on your résumé.

Exaggeration *is* lying.

> Lies on your résumé can go undiscovered for decades and then, upon their sudden revelation, can get you kicked to the curb without severance.

Some companies, particularly those in the high-tech sector, prefer to receive résumés in electronic form.

While it is true that most of those high-tech companies are now shuttered and selling off their dry-erase boards for pennies on the dollar and thus are of no concern, it doesn't hurt to inquire as to a company's predilections, résumé-wise.

References: You ask someone if he's willing to vouch for you before listing him as a reference.

What to do when a prospective employer calls to ask about someone who has listed you as a reference without your permission: Recall the applicant's fondness for taxidermy, his desktop ant farm, and his garlicky homemade hummus.

When someone agrees to serve as a reference, send him a thank-you note and a copy of your résumé, the latter so he'll be up to speed on your doings.

Use discretion in the number of employers to whom you give your references' names, so that they are not inundated with calls about you.

Three words for when a reference is inundated with calls about you: taxidermy, ants, hummus.

When you show up for the interview: Be on time.

Definition of "on time": exactly five minutes early, no less, no more.

This definition, by the way, applies to all business appointments.

There are those who believe punctuality is the key to success—that, of course, and not soiling one's undergarments at meetings.

Punctuality is one of those things that we in the scientific community like to call a "necessary but not sufficient condition" for success.

At the interview: Wear classic business attire.

Because dressing like a Phish fan is a stupid thing to do even at a Phish *concert*, and you are not presently in attendance at a Phish concert.

More on classic business attire later.

Don't smoke in the office, nor immediately outside the office, nor within 30 minutes of approaching the office, or you will smell like a smoker—and virtually nobody likes a smoker anymore.

For that matter: Don't smoke at all, if possible, smoking having been discovered to be fatal.

Two words: breath mints.

When you show up for the interview: Behave perfectly and cordially from the moment you enter the reception area, and particularly be polite to the receptionist.

In re the previous: Know that most job interviewers will ask their assistant what the assistant thought of you.

And if you treated the assistant like a dung beetle, she is going to tell your prospective employer that you are an ass and an imbecile.

22

Don't sit down until you are directed to sit down.

You see, you want not to indicate to your prospective employers that you run the place until you are hired and, in fact, run the place.

23

Chapter three

What are my strengths and weaknesses? Well, for starters, I have a weakness for authority figures who hold my destiny in the oily palms of their dirty little hands

When the interviewer asks for your strengths and weaknesses, the one and only weakness you cite is a weakness that you formerly had, but have since completely conquered.

Example of an appropriate weakness: excessive attention to keeping things organized, perhaps sometimes at the expense of creative thinking, which you now consider very important.

Weaknesses you won't be mentioning: cherry wine, cheroots, Casper the Friendly Ghost, high school gymnasts, Thai stick, pajama bottoms with footies, the fantastical mustaches on glorious display during those delicious, bourbon-soaked Tuesdays at the Ukrainian baths.

When he asks your current salary: Know that nobody, interviewers included, has any right to know your current salary.

In re the previous: You don't, of course, say it like that.

While we're on the subject of compensation secrecy: People who especially have no right to know your salary are your current coworkers, whose reactions can only be resentment or pity. Tell no one.

When you learn someone's salary inadvertently, such as that time you spotted someone's paycheck on her desk and simply couldn't help reading it: Tell no one.

Especially don't tell your boss that you know what she's paying other people when you're angling for a raise. Because it will make her angry. Because she will ask where you got your information.

When a job interviewer asks your current salary: Try to divert the conversation to the salary range for this position.

If she dodges and asks again: Say something to the effect that you and your current employer have an agreement that your compensation package will be kept confidential, and isn't the issue really about how well a fit you are for this company and this spot right here and right now.

A scenario.

Interviewer: So, Johnson, what are they paying you over at Stainblot?

> **Applicant:** Well, Mr. Mister, I take my salary in buffy-headed marmosets, so it's hard to translate—say, what *is* the salary range for this position, anyhoo?

27

Another scenario.

Interviewer: So, Johnson, what are they paying you over at Stainblot?

Applicant: Well, Mr. Mister, while I would be happy to provide you with my salary history at the appropriate point in our discussions, it strikes me that my current rate has little bearing on my future compensation requirements, which are $X,XXX,XXX.00—that *is* consistent with the range for this position, right?

The previous tactic is a bit aggressive but has among its virtues an admirably straightforward quality.

Then again, another school of thought holds that the first person to name a figure in any negotiation has already lost, because the other side may have been willing to pay more (or accept less).

In any negotiation, the first person to say "anyhoo" loses.

Finally, know this: The buffy-headed marmoset is native to Brazil and is gravely endangered and it is probably in poor professional taste to take one's compensation in imperiled jungle creatures.

Just FYI.

After the interview, if you haven't heard back: Wait one week and two days, then call to "check in."

Which reminds us—you know that gesture where you make quotation marks with your fingers as you speak certain words? Don't do that.

No, it's not a point of etiquette. It just makes you look stupid.

When you get the job: Keep your head down and your voice soft for a time, because you are fresh meat, and fresh meat is as vulnerable as a soft and fuzzy lamb.

When you're fresh meat: Keep quiet about your personal life, at least until you've figured out who is trustworthy and who is a rat.

Mr. Etiquette Man!

Question: If I'm expecting an important call, is it okay to leave my cell phone on during a meeting?

Answer: Yes. That is why Mr. Bell invented the "vibrate" mode. (If your phone does not vibrate, the answer would be no, followed by this advice: Your phone is old and should be replaced at once.)

Question: Is it okay to *answer* my cell phone in the meeting?

Answer: Yes, of *course* it's okay, because you are the one, the only, Academy Award–winning actress and America's Sweetheart, Julia Roberts! Oh—you're not Julia Roberts? You must excuse yourself and step well out of earshot to take your calls.

Chapter four

We've got your workday casual—right here: Clothes do, it turns out, make the man

Your clothes are the first thing people notice about you.

At least, they are now that you've removed that barbell piercing from your eyebrow.

As most employers do not want people to notice that their employees are Green Day enthusiasts who do a lot of faux finishing when they are not hiking Tiddlypom Gorge, it would be best not to wear concert T-shirts, paint-stained pants, or trail boots to the office.

Call us traditionalists.

The nontraditionalists? You can call them, too, most likely at home, where they've been watching *Judge Judy* since their dot-com died.

Something else to keep in mind: No one ever got ignored, denied a promotion, or refused a raise because they wore a suit or sport coat to work.

The sport coat: You should accompany that with a pair of trousers, huh?

All trousers need not be khakis.

As pertains to footwear: leather and suede lace-ups and loafers.

While, strictly speaking, sandals are shoes, they are not shoes.

To those who think suits and ties and sport coats are restrictive and inhibit creative thinking: Edison didn't need Dockers to do what he did with the lightbulb. And the phonograph. And the stock ticker.

> Plus: Suits and ties and sport coats are not uncomfortable. Cheap or ill-fitting suits and ties and sport coats are uncomfortable.

The Empty Suit: A useless lump who nonetheless manages to prosper at work because he always looks good.

You see, there is no shame in dressing well for work.

35

Dressing well for work directly translates to your eventually making more money than you otherwise would.

The thing is, the clothes *do* make the man.

A slight aside: The clothes that make the man often attract the woman, which, while having nothing to do with etiquette, might be something to keep in mind. Especially if you're single.

ask
Mr. Etiquette Man!

Question: What do you wear to a "black-tie optional" event?

Answer: In our book, there should be no such thing as a "black-tie optional" event—such a designation serves only to confuse us all. Most men take it to mean they can show up in their business suit and battered wing tips, which, we suppose, they can. But that means they're guaranteeing from the beginning that they will be the least elegant men in the room, because probably more than half the attendees will wear tuxedos, and thus will look superior. So: Wear a tuxedo, or, if that feels wrong for the circumstances, an elegant black suit with a white shirt and a solid black tie—and, in any case, wear well-shined shoes.

If you think you must wear cologne or aftershave, you're mistaken.

Use all the mouthwash and breath mints you like.

You know that fish tie you should not wear anywhere at all, ever, no matter the circumstances (unless of course you work for Ringling Brothers)? You should particularly not wear it to work.

Put another way: How many CEOs and Nobel laureates and rising star executives have you observed wearing fish ties?

Yes, exactly our point.

Chapter five

The Long March, aka Bataan via Camry, aka the commute

Know that you are not the only person coping with the dawn of another workday mired in depression and grief—no, no, that would be everybody.

Now, then: Cheer up and quit griping if, indeed, you have a job, as it is still morning and traditionally many managers wait until the afternoon to fire people.

If you carpool, don't bring coffee.

Because other people will wish A) that they, too, had a fragrant, steaming cuppa, or B) that you were not posing such a grave threat to their upholstery, or C), and most important, that their reproductive area was not blistering from the effects of spilled scalding liquid.

All energy savings aside, you really don't want to be involved in a car pool.

To spell it out: Your weekend is dead and gone, your noggin is throbbing, and five days of head-spinning fiduciary riddles loom dead ahead—do you really want to kick off the week crammed into a Toyota full of yammering coworkers?

Similarly, urban types: The train ride to work is for reading, not talking.

Especially not talking on the cell phone.

Because the other passengers want to read Esquire or sleep or (bafflingly) stare blankly into dark train windows without any reading material at all, not listen to your self-important bloviating.

The other passengers probably should not be privy to the transaction of your business anyway.

And they should be even less privy to personal conversations.

Of course, we could write a whole book on cell-phone etiquette, but it all comes down to this: You know how when you hear someone nattering on their Nokia and you want to take it and stick it where its only useful function might be the vibrating answer mode? People feel that way about you, too.

What to do: Keep cell calls short.

Conduct cell calls in places where others aren't forced to listen.

And before you place each cell call, think about how you once got along fine without being in constant communication with everybody.

Chapter six

Life in the cubicle (and the hallway and the break room and the supply closet)

Now then: Are we all at our desks? Good. We begin.

Face time: Those hours in which your superiors and coworkers see that you are, indeed, physically at the workplace and apparently on the job.

Face time is not worth much if you have shown up late.

Calling in sick: Unless you are a person with an established and proven record of chronic ill health, calling in sick is kept to a minimum.

> **People who are thought to be calling in sick when they are not sick will be considered untrustworthy, whiny, and weak.**

However: When you truly do have a communicable illness, you call in sick not so much to heal thyself but to spare your coworkers.

Speaking of calls: There is a right way and a wrong way to answer the telephone at the office, and the wrong way is, "Hello?"

The really, really wrong way—the kind of wrong that makes us reverse our position on cooling-off periods for firearms: scripted hellos that feature sales spiels.

Example: "Thank you for calling Stainblot, Inc., where protein-based fluids don't stand a chance against Spot-a-Lot! detergent. How may I direct your call?"

In re the previous, someone at every company is responsible for telling receptionists what to say when they answer the phone; if this someone is you, you have the power to stop such abuse with one memo.

If your company's phones are first answered by a voice-mail system, it is a new requirement under FCC Code 57-2231 Subsection XXIIVI that this system must immediately and at any time allow callers to reach a human operator by pressing zero.

Well, it *should* be a requirement.

The right way to answer your own phone: Simply speak your name— "Hello, Verzetti here."

The right way to answer your boss's phone: "Mr. Potemkin's office."

The way to answer your own phone when you don't want people to know they've reached your direct line: "Stainblot, Inc."

Especially if your company is not called Stainblot, Inc.

When you're calling somebody important and busy, an excellent opening line is as follows: "Is this a good time?"

Excellent response when the answer to that question is no: "I'll pop off an e-mail and try you back later."

After which time you pop off an e-mail so the important party doesn't forget you called, and then you call back later.

Not ten minutes later. Three or four hours later.

When a phone conversation is the first time you've ever spoken to someone, you could probably be forgiven for saying, "Nice to meet you," because they're going to know what you mean. However, you have not actually met them.

Better to say, "It was a pleasure speaking with you."

You know those people who are nearly impossible to get off the phone, and who become so widely known as such that nobody wants to take their calls, and who, as a direct result of this inappropriate response to loneliness and desperation, suffer the actual economic damages of lost business? Don't be one of those people.

The biggest favor you can do for the previously referenced person—and for yourself: Tell them they're too difficult to get off the phone.

Why this is a favor for yourself: In future, as they hear themselves talking too much, they may learn to cut themselves off.

How to get someone off the phone: Glance at your watch and react with genuine alarm, exclaiming something along the lines of "Great horny toads—sorry to interrupt you, but I was supposed to be in a budget meeting ten minutes ago!"

(Yes, we know the person on the other end can't see you glance at your watch. Think of it as Method acting.)

And then: Thank the caller for calling, and tell her you'll be in touch.

**We didn't literally mean you should say,
"Great horny toads."**

Everybody loves really
short voice-mail messages.

**Everybody hates really
long voice-mail messages.**

On your outgoing voice-mail message, you don't need
to say that you can't come to the phone right now,
because, well, if you could we wouldn't be listening to
your outgoing voice-mail message.

Ninety-nine percent of all voice-mail messages need contain solely your name, your company name, your number, and the request for a call back.

> **Speakerphone? What are you, a Hollywood agent or something?**

> **Speaking of which, babe: One does not *do* lunch. One *has* lunch. "Would you like to have lunch?" Like that.**

When using a speakerphone with multiple people in the room, you must immediately inform the party you're calling that there are other people in the room.

More on telephone tech: The ubiquity of caller ID must be borne in mind before you attempt to lie about where you're calling from (especially those of you prone to calling in sick from, say, Disney World).

Or before you make crank calls to the chairman of the board.

What an assistant says when the boss is in a meeting: "I'm sorry, she's in a meeting, may I take a message?"

What an assistant says when the boss is not in a meeting but nonetheless wants to be left alone: "I'm sorry, she's in a meeting, may I take a message?"

Some people in this situation pronounce the word "message" as "massage," but fortunately not too many, and none of them is you.

Use proper grammar and clear speech—and do not attempt to eat doughnuts while talking on the phone.

Fairly or not, strong regional or foreign accents can be a hindrance to your career. You might consider a few sessions with a voice coach.

Chapter seven

I'm mad as hell, and I'm going to salve my rage in a soothing chat with one of several thousand disinterested phone reps—yeah, that's the ticket

Calls from angry and irrational people: What you do is you allow the aggrieved party to blow off steam, to rage and holler and fume, without taking it personally, offering soothing interjections such as "Mmm-hmm" and "I'm sorry this has been such trouble for you," and things like that.

Executives who use their secretaries to place calls for them and who won't pick up until the party they're calling is on the line—these executives look a lot less important than they think they do.

If you're on the receiving end of one of these calls: Feel no need to remain on hold for more than thirty seconds before hanging up.

Personal calls: Obviously, they're not why you're here, and thus ought be kept to a minimum.

Visits by spouse and children: best confined to brief, after-hours walk-throughs and Take Your Child to Work days, if then.

On second thought, your kid will be taking his own damned self to work all too soon—leave the rugrat at home.

When communication takes written form: 95 percent of all business correspondence begins with the words "Thank you."

Ninety-five percent of all requests you make of staffers and colleagues employs the word "Please."

The business letter: Current workplace mores find it just a bit too insouciant to dot the *i*'s with little hearts.

The business letter: Never commit strong feelings, especially those pertaining to love and anger, to paper, especially not letterhead.

You don't want to do this with e-mail, either.

Most letters, including business letters, begin with the word "Dear," as in "Dear Mr. Jablonski."

Business letters should be as brief and to the point as possible.

Business letters that are not brief and to the point are much less likely to be effective or to spark a timely response—if only because it takes more time to craft a response to a complicated missive.

Signing off: Very truly yours, Regards, or Best.

You could try Sincerely, but, when it comes to business, you should try not to lie more often than necessary.

Brightly colored sticky notes and unusual paper clips are for teenage girls.

Sticky notes are not stationery.

Nor are e-mails.

When an e-mail suffices as a thank-you note: rarely—usually when you're thanking a close friend or family member.

Mr. Etiquette Man!

ask

Question: When should I send thank-you notes?

Answer: When someone interviews you for a job, takes you out for a meal or drinks, gives you a gift (even a small, crummy, corporate gift), interviews you for a magazine or newspaper, serves as a reference, a house sitter or a dog walker—in short, virtually any time that virtually anybody does virtually anything nice for you.

Question: But come on—nobody sends thank-you notes just because someone bought them a drink, do they?

Answer: You are correct, in the main. *Almost* nobody does. Those few who do, they are remembered and admired and seen as the true class acts they are.

Corporate stationery is an important element of your company's identity and should be high quality.

There is no upside to telling a coworker they look as if they've lost weight or gained weight.

On weight-related compliments: For starters, weight-loss or -gain often results from horrible illnesses you really don't want to be talking about.

On weight-related compliments: They also reveal to coworkers that you very well might have been "checking out" areas of their physical form that you have no business checking out.

Eating at your desk is to be avoided.

Because food is smelly and eating is a different thing from working and working is really the sort of thing you want your coworkers to associate with you, no?

When lunch must involve your desk: Move aside contracts and files and presentation graphics before you whip out the hoagie, and after said hoagie is dispatched, give the desk a good wiping-down.

Never eat anything called a "hoagie."

When lunch must involve eating at your desk: It is kindly to avoid particularly smelly food, particularly if nearby workers would be subjected to the aroma.

It is wise to avoid food that will adversely affect the character of your breath.

It is very wise to avoid food that has any externally discernible impact on your body—turning your tongue red, say, or reminding anybody of that scene from *Blazing Saddles*.

If you toss the remains of that fish taco in your own trash can, you and your colleagues will smell it the rest of the day—better to discard it upstairs in Accounting.

The previous item, while true, was a joke, and in fact contravenes the whole idea of etiquette being about—uh-huh—respect.

After lunch: The toothbrush, if possible; the mouthwash, a close second; the breath mint, at minimum.

Gum chewing: No.

Put another way, note the number of CEOs and Nobel laureates and rising star executives you have observed chewing gum on the job.

Yes, exactly our point.

Neither singing nor whistling are sounds one employs in the workplace, with the possible exception of a workplace that is a polka hall.

Likewise, playing a music CD on your computer is an activity best avoided.

And it doesn't have to be a Rammstein CD for people to feel that way.

To certain folks, Anne Murray can be just as upsetting as a German death-metal group.

Not a solution: headphones.

Because headphones indicate that you're more interested in hearing the Singing Sweetheart of Spring Hill, Nova Scotia, warble about snowbirds or looking at life from both sides now than you are in hearing about the boss's next project.

On the walls in many large corporations, there hang framed posters featuring photographs of landscape scenes, sometimes emblazoned with motivational exhortations, such as "Success: One customer at a time."

It is ill-advised to take a gigantic Sharpie and scrawl the profane things you'd like to do to those customers, one at a time or perhaps in groups, on these posters.

Because this is the office. You don't get to decorate it.

68

If, on the other hand, you are a human-resources professional and you *do* get to decorate it: Do not, under any circumstances, waste corporate resources on such condescending posters—thank you.

Metallica posters: if you're an ad-agency creative under 28 or you work for Metallica's record label.

Dilbert ephemera: That's original.

Chapter eight

This liverwurst sandwich property of Lucine Kasbarian—do not touch!!!!!!

Everybody who drinks the office coffee should occasionally make a pot.

Notice that the previous item did not say, "All the *women* who drink the office coffee," but, rather, "everybody."

"Everybody" might include the big boss in some offices and definitely does not in others, and are you going to be the one to call him on it if he's skulking off with the last cup all day long? No. You are not.

Never leave angry public notes.

Especially never leave angry public notes concerning such trivialities as the fact that everybody who drinks the office coffee should occasionally make a pot, but, sadly, does not do so.

Instead of leaving a note: Photocopy a page from an authoritative third party, such as this very book, and affix same in the appropriate place.

Conduct the following activities not at your desk but, rather, in the washroom: hair combing, teeth brushing, makeup slathering, nail buffing, tongue scraping (shudder).

Regarding tongue maintenance: Make that your bathroom at home, preferably that one way off in the guest cabana, where we'll not have to know about it.

Don't bring papers, reports, memos, or ledgers into the men's room with you.

Why not? Well, for one thing, they're hard to wash, those ledgers.

If for some reason you have to bring papers, reports, memos, or ledgers into the men's room with you, leave them outside the stall.

> On second thought, that's not an acceptable option, because someone could riffle through or steal your documents—which is to say (is there an echo in here?), don't bring papers, reports, memos, or ledgers into the men's room with you.

Upon leaving the stall, one washes one's hands. This occurs before picking up the papers, reports, memos, or ledgers.

And this occurs whether you have company in the men's room or not.

Under no circumstances should you leave the stall and announce, "Boy, oh, boy, that's the last time I order the chicken vindaloo, I can tell you that much."

Here's another idea: Do whatever it is you would do in the stall at home before you come to work.

Yes, you see, as once literally spelled out in a hit song by a certain full-figured lady of Motown fame: Respect.

You don't have to pitch in every time someone takes up a collection for a coworker's baby shower.

ask Mr. Etiquette Man!

Question: What do you do when you've accidentally sent a sensitive, potentially damaging e-mail to the wrong person?

Answer: Pray with every fiber of your being that the recipient has not yet read the missive. Then, if there's any way to swing past the recipient's desk and delete the message yourself (and don't forget the Trash queue also), do so. Otherwise, you hope that the recipient has an assistant, and that the assistant has access to the recipient's e-mail password. And now: It's times like this when you truly see why it's so important to be kind to support staff, because you're going to call this assistant, and you're going to explain that you've made a terrible mistake, and that innocent people could be harmed and untold profits lost, and you're going to ask her to delete the message for you. Failing this, you've little choice but to call the recipient, lay it on the line, tell them the message was intended for someone else, and ask them to erase it. If they've seen it and found it insulting or offensive, take responsibility, apologize, and tell them you wrote the note in anger or passion. Thank-you notes would very much be in order here, as would, in some cases, a bouquet of flowers and/or the performance of hara-kiri.

You don't have to participate in the football pool.

You don't have to play "Secret Santa."

Regarding the previous office rituals, declining to participate may get you labeled as aloof.

There are worse things than being called aloof.

Among them: getting fired for neglecting your widget-selling duties in favor of baby showers, football pools, and Secret Santa preparations.

Should you find yourself accused of aloofness, open this book to this very page, hold it before your accuser, and point to the following item:

Nobody in this room is receiving monetary compensation to fill their lonely hours with such time-wasting frippery as baby showers, football pools, and Secret Santa extravaganzas, and, while you may choose to do so anyway, some of us have ambition and families to feed and an actual work ethic—thus, would you kindly allow me to get back to work? Thank you.

Better still: *Think* the aforementioned item without actually communicating it, and spend the five bucks it will cost to make your coworker go away. To our minds, that's five bucks well spent.

Chapter nine

It's 11:37 and we're damned pleased to meet you

Hot on the heels of the handshake, importance-wise: the introductions.

Approaching a stranger to inquire, "I'm Joe Strummer, and _you_ are...?" is the introductory equivalent to "Who the hell are _you_?"

As a general principle, the format of the introductions should involve introducing less-important people to more-important people.

Furthermore, those introductions are phrased to reflect the fact that less-important persons should consider the introduction a privilege.

Correctly formatted introduction: Genevieve, I think you'll recognize my wife, Jennifer Lopez; Jennifer, may I present Genevieve Bouchon, my Parisian mistress?

Correctly formatted introduction: Mr. President, I'd like my daughter, Mavis Leventhal, to meet you; Mavis, this is Mr. G.W. Braintree, our nation's 43rd president.

Incorrectly formatted introduction: Mick, I'd like you to meet Schlomo Kottke, my cousin with the klezmer operation outta Philly; Schlomo, this is Mick Jagger—he's a singer, too!

Tough-call introduction: Larry King to Phyllis Diller. Or is it Phyllis Diller to Larry King?

Introducing yourself *by name*, even to people who should remember who you are, is the gentlemanly thing to do.

Because everybody, including people who shouldn't—including yourself—forgets people's names now and then.

Deliberately making others squirm for failing to remember your name is spiteful.

When you forget someone's name: Attempt to overhear them introduce themselves to others.

Failing that, when you forget someone's name: Confess immediately, apologize, and attribute your mistake to stress over your recent IRS audit and that cranial-surgery episode.

Pop quiz: What was wrong with the previous item?

81

Answer: You never, ever discuss in public anything to do with personal financial matters or your health (topics that are, respectively, awkward to offensive, and sad to nauseating). Instead, just confess your forgetfulness and apologize and stop. There.

If you repeatedly forget the same person's name, however, you're pretty clearly telegraphing the possibility that you find them less than crucially important.

Then again, don't feel bad: Not so many people *are* crucially important.

Business cards are for handing out at business functions.

Not at social functions.

Business functions: meetings, conventions, strategic luncheons, job interviews, plant visits.

Social functions: dates, church services, your daughter's school play, state dinners.

Business cards are one and three quarter inches high and three and a half inches wide, period.

They are not decorated with photos of you or drawings of animals.

On the subject of names: no nicknames.

On the subject of the prohibition of nicknames: Is your workplace a fraternal organization, such as those on the campuses of large universities, where boisterous young fellows drink beer from great plastic cups and dress as Romans? No, it is not.

On the subject of the prohibition of nicknames: That goes double for you, Mister Leader of the Free World.

(FYI: Fidel likes to be called Señor Happypants.)

Names you shouldn't use for colleagues, regardless of their junior-executive status: kid, kiddo, junior, punky, boo-boo.

Because nobody wants to be called kid, kiddo, junior, punky, or boo-boo, and seeing as how you're fully aware of your seniority and the munchkins are fully aware of your seniority, who, exactly are you trying to impress here?

Come to think, we find boo-boo kind of cute. Call us boo-boo. Thank you.

The word *cute* is used only in reference to puppies and children.

Generally, the boss is not addressed as "Boss."

"Boss" has a certain chain-gang overtone that, while perhaps applicable, may not be something your boss wants to be reminded about.

Because she's the boss.

Because she's the big-man alpha-dog 800-pound kahuna-huna hooey.

Because she wears the proverbial pants—the boogly-boogly pants!

We'll explain these pants later.

The boss is also not addressed as "Dude."

The boss is not addressed as "Dude" even if the boss likes to be addressed as "Dude"—perhaps especially so--because such behavior can only perpetuate a culture of extravagant "Dude" usage up and down the organizational chart.

The other reason the boss doesn't want you calling her nicknames: She must maintain a certain level of detachment from you so that she can fire you if necessary.

Calling her "Dude" will not prevent her from firing you.

Speaking of firing, dot-com refugees are to be regarded with sympathy, not derision.

Because there is nothing wrong with taking risks in the seeking of one's fortune.

Refugees of the Internet bubble are not to be referred to as "e-holes."

On second thought: The risks taken by most e-holes chiefly involved money that was not their own; plus, they called their bosses "Dude" and wore sandals to the office.

All this by way of advice to former "new-economy" e-holes trying once again to make their way in the "old economy," which it now appears is actually the only economy: Hope you were nice to people on your way up, because you're seeing them on the way down, aren't you? Yes.

Chapter ten

Your gal Friday, who, chances are better than fifty-fifty, might prefer not to be called a "gal"

Being that one of the chief secrets of a successful career is to make the support staff love you: Always greet your gal Friday with a smile and a genuine good morning.

On the use of the term "gal Friday": only as a humor device, and only if it can be convincingly demonstrated later in a harassment lawsuit that all sides understood the humor.

Which is to say, in most cases, the use of terms like "gal Friday" is not a good program.

In fact, neither gender is especially well served by the use of such terms as "Babe" or "Honey" or "Sweet Peachy Bottom," and those who employ them should be instructed to instead use people's actual names.

More important than an MBA: an understanding of the importance of assistants as sources of intelligence and know-how, and how to make them happy.

How to make assistants happy, step one: Notice that they exist.

An aside: The aforementioned rule applies to human beings in general.

How to make assistants happy, step two: Having noticed their existence, recognize that their worth as human beings is exactly equal to your own, even possibly greater, and speak to them in tones that convey friendliness and respect.

How to make assistants happy, part three: While not mandatory, the occasional modest gift or help with a heavy parcel or definitely nonsexual compliment on clothing does not hurt.

Caveat: Establish dominance quickly.

Because you don't want to find yourself in a situation like Drew Carey and that woman with the makeup.

Limit the number of drinks you consume and the amount of time you spend with employees below your station.

The aforementioned does *not* mean it is acceptable to be unkind to or look down upon employees who rank lower than you do; it is a part of the professional detachment you must preserve, just as your boss does over you, in the case of needing to discipline someone.

It's about order and discipline and limits—all of which allow an office to function more smoothly than one in which the assistants call their bosses "Dude-sicle"—such as in the Army, where the officers have their own mess and their own nightclub, you see.

People who are rude to support staff receive the attendant dislike of support staff—and then, when the chips are down, they discover how badly they need the support staff.

Regarding your secretary: Don't
call him your secretary.

Also don't call him "boy."

Though if he is a female, it might be amusing to
call your secretary "boy."

If possible, see to it that your secretary receives
a new title along the lines of "administrative assistant"
or "personal assistant" or "department coordinator" or
"assistant to the King," where the King is you, or some
such.

Personal errands: The extent to which your assistant should be running personal errands for you depends on many factors, among them his expertise and experience, your seniority, but, most important, the agreed-upon responsibilities his position entails.

For example, the executive aide to the CEO of Sony does not run out for sandwiches; she phones up a lesser secretary or messenger who then runs out for sandwiches.

The assistant to Bob, the manager of Coconuts Records and Tapes at Olde Orchard Centre, might reasonably be expected to procure Bob's Subway Club.

When it is okay to expect your secretary to pick up your dry cleaning: when your secretary was hired with the understanding that he would now and then pick up your dry cleaning.

Or when you ask really nicely and he agrees without hesitation.

Regarding sex with an assistant: so long as it is somebody else's assistant.

From a different firm.

In another city.

When you are called upon to help an unimpressive underling find work elsewhere via a recommendation you'd rather not provide, it is better to say you don't know enough about the person than it is to trash them.

Which, by the way, is the same thing as trashing them, only it's not "actionable."

Which isn't to say you should praise without reserve someone you do like: Your reputation, in such cases, is affected by their behavior once they get the job.

How to give a recommendation: Make a brief list of the person's positive attributes and recite that list over the telephone.

After twelve months in your employ, your assistant will know more about you than you know about yourself.

This can make her either excellent counsel or your worst enemy. Which is up to you.

It is, once again, a matter of respect.

How she can be your worst enemy: She can unveil your shadings of the truth, disseminate your bad-mouthing, and lay bare your practice of filching Post-Its and paper clips for home use.

Mr. Etiquette Man!

ask

Question: When I'm using a speakerphone, is it necessary to tell the person I'm calling that there are other people in the room?

Answer: It is absolutely necessary, unless you are conducting hostage negotiations or if you want the boss to discover that his staff calls him "Orca." You should also know this: When you're on a speakerphone, your every cough, burp, keystroke and rustling comic-book page is amplified and duly noted on the other end of the line.

In the office, there should be no shadings of the truth.

Except, of course, for the obviously necessary types of truth-shading.

There should be no bad-mouthing.

There should be no gossiping.

Put another way: How many CEOs and Nobel laureates and rising star executives have you observed whispering about which manager is shtupping whom?

Yes, exactly our point.

True, this sharing is something we humans like to do. It can make life easier, make us feel better about ourselves, make us tingle with the fresh joy of discovery. No one disputes that. It is just inadvisable if you wish to remain comfortably employed.

One other thing, above all, that there should not be: hanky-panky with your gal Friday.

Why? Hoo-boy!

As pertains to other staff: The same rules of conduct that apply to your G.F. should apply to them. And also this:

Listen.

Understand.

Encourage.

Inspire.

Allow them a certain amount of autonomy in their jobs.

Praise them when they do well.

If you are a manager of people, it is essential to bestow a certain amount of praise upon those people, or they will eventually shoot themselves—or you.

When you're about to be shot, etiquette dictates that you throw up your hands, scream like a Canadian figure skater, and run like hell.

Wetting your pants is an acceptable option, but by no means necessary.

Back to your staff: Gently discipline them when they do ill.

When we speak of discipline, we don't mean the kind administered by an English schoolmistress in horn-rimmed glasses and knickers.

Sadly.

Discipline should take place privately.

Discipline should proceed on the presumption that Sully, say, has made a small error and because he is a good and smart man—would you have hired him if he were not?—you both understand that he will make no future small errors.

Also, listen to his response to your concern. He may have a good excuse.

Generally, excuses are like opinions: Everyone has one and most are wrong. Still, it doesn't hurt to hear it.

Discipline is best delivered with a bedrock of praise.

See, the idea is to create an environment for your subordinates that you, if you were a subordinate, would like to work within every day for the next thirty years.

Hit it, Aretha: *R-e-s-p-e-c-t.*

Chapter eleven
The three-Pellegrino lunch

A lunch meeting is an appointment, and an appointment is a time-related event to which one is not late.

Period.

Also, one is not too early.

> The reason you don't want to be early: When the rest of your party arrives, you'll look like somebody with time on his hands—and therefore with less authority and responsibility than the rest of your party.

You'll also feel sorry for yourself, sitting there forlornly, twirling an empty wineglass, trying not to feel jilted.

What to be: on time.

If you are late—if, say, your cab has been caught behind the circus parade—call the restaurant and ask them to let your dining companions know.

Yes, this is one of the few appropriate uses for a cell phone, after which you will put it away and not use it again until after the lunch.

Away means turned off and lodged securely in your pocket or bag, and not on the table where you might be tempted to spin it round and round.

Whoever proposed the lunch pays for the lunch.

The previous item holds true regardless of either party's age, rank, or gender.

When proposing a lunch or dinner, determine from the outset whether any guests have complicated diets or intense political leanings as regard food, and select the restaurant accordingly.

That does not mean you take Serbians to the Croatian Café, or that you take vegans to Sizzler, although that sounds like a tickle. What it means is exactly the opposite of that, smartypants.

It is a warm gesture to take foreign visitors to a place that serves food they'll appreciate and understand—a place that serves the cuisine of their homeland, perhaps.

It's often a good idea to select a restaurant where the staff knows you and where your connectedness might impress your guests. Just don't be overbearing or showy about it.

If circumstances make it too difficult to ascertain personal culinary data: Select a restaurant that's not exotic or controversial (with Americans, you can't go wrong with Italian) and that features a widely varied menu.

But watch that splattery spaghetti.

Also: You could ask your guests beforehand what sorts of food they'd like. They might have a powerful hankering for fried chicken.

Traditionally, you don't talk business until dessert and coffee.

What you talk about before dessert: families, hobbies, sports, people's houses, hometowns, career trajectories, upcoming vacations—in short, the same things you talk about when getting to know anybody personally.

What you don't talk about: your health, your SugarBusters diet, your debt, your politics, faith-based anything, the Middle East, how bad the food is, your boss's hot wife.

Your napkin goes into your lap the moment you sit down.

When you get up to take a phone call or to use the bathroom, you leave your napkin on your chair, not on the table.

Because no one wants to see your wrinkled, stained linen next to his swordfish carpaccio.

ask Mr. Etiquette Man!

Question: What does fine wine service look like?

Answer: a) The sommelier shows the bottle to the host to confirm that she's getting the wine she asked for. The sommelier uncorks the bottle and hands the cork to the host, who inspects the cork for dryness or crumbling and verifies that the cork is imprinted with the correct château or brand. Many people sniff the cork, but not you, because you know that there is nothing you can learn from sniffing the cork that you can't learn better from sniffing the wine. Plus, it looks stupid.

b) The sommelier pours a small amount into the glass of the host, who smells it (without an audible inhale) and tastes it with a minimum of fuss and bother (and certainly no gurgling), and nods her approval.

c) If the host disapproves—that is, if she believes the wine has gone bad because of improper storage or a faulty cork (the wine is "corked")—she should quietly mention this problem to the sommelier, who must also taste the wine to see if he agrees. If he does, the bottle will be replaced without charge.

d) The host knows better than to reject a bottle of wine if she doesn't know what she's talking about.

Note to those waiters who snap up napkins from chairs, refold them, and place them back on the table: Don't. Again, leave it on the chair.

Feel free to have a glass of wine at a business lunch, particularly if others at the table are doing so.

Do not feel free to have a second glass of wine.

Regarding the wine: Don't talk about it.

Even if you're the consummate authority on Sauternes.
Especially so, in fact.

What to do when someone asks you to select the wine and you're *not* the consummate authority on Sauternes: Discreetly signal your waiter, tell him what people have ordered, and ask for his recommendation.

What to do when the waiter asks for your price range, wine-wise: Point to an entry on the wine list.

Wineglasses are shaped the way they are shaped in order to best concentrate the aromas beneath your nose.

The miniature wineglass is for cordials, sherry, or dessert wine.

You really needn't worry about the glasses. That's what waiters are for.

When it comes to the food, never order anything that is difficult to eat.

Because nobody wants to shake
a greasy hand.

Because the contract isn't going to the
guy who's licking hollandaise off his tie.

Because slurping spaghettini out your nose is
unlikely to get you a raise.

**(Admittedly, there may be some lines of work in
which the ability to slurp spaghettini out one's nose
might get one a raise.)**

Mr. Etiquette Man!

Question: How do I ask for a raise?

Answer: First, consider honestly whether you truly deserve one. No—*honestly*, we said. It doesn't matter that you want more money; most people do. It doesn't matter much that coworkers are making more than you are; that generally means that your boss considers them more valuable or experienced (although it might just mean they are "squeakier wheels"—that is, that they've gone to the trouble to ask for more money). Now then: Go in with evidence (no charts, no graphs, but a few firm figures in your head). Talk of recent accomplishments, awards you've won, increases in your responsibility, increases in the number of employees you oversee or clients you maintain or widgets you have sold. Stay positive and friendly. Speak of your desire to grow with the organization. Then, when the big guy comes across with a handsome boost, write him a thank-you note and forward an appropriate cut to the authors of this book, care of our publishers. Fifteen percent would do nicely. Thank you.

Foods to avoid at a business luncheon: hollandaise, French onion soup, barbecued ribs, salads of unchopped greens in splatter-prone vinaigrette, anything you would hold in your hands and bite pieces from, anything involving hundreds of tiny bones, anything involving copious amounts of brightly colored sauce.

Speaking of copious amounts, a business lunch is not the place to demonstrate how much you can pack down your gullet.

When you bite down on a piece of gristle: Discreetly take in a deep breath, so as to attract as little attention as possible, and, having used your tongue to move the gristle to the front of your mouth, just behind the lips, expel it with a sharp burst of air toward the best-looking woman at the table. Then, look surprised.

The authors of this book are completely at a loss as to the presence of the previous entry.

Here's how it's really done: When you bite down on a piece of gristle, lift your napkin or spoon to your lips as if preparing to dab or take a sip of soup, and, all the while acting natural so as not to draw attention, convey the item down to the rim of your plate.

The cutlery placed horizontally above your plate—that is, where the twelve would be if your plate were a clock—that cutlery is for dessert.

The small fork is for salad, unless it's a funny-looking small fork, in which case it's for extracting seafood from its shell (which you shouldn't be doing anyway, per earlier advice, because of the splatter problem).

Similarly, the funny-looking knife, should there be one, is for fish.

The small knife is for bread.

The big spoon is for soup.

> Not the big spoon that's in the whipped parsnips—that's for serving the whipped parsnips.

All you really need to know about which fork goes where: The cutlery you should be using for each course will be the cutlery farthest from either side of the plate during that course.

Scientific fact: Nobody is paying the slightest attention to which fork you're using, unless you've stuck it into your head.

In the rare instance that someone is paying attention, they are thinking one of two things: a) that they, themselves, are using the wrong fork, or b) that you are from Europe.

If they should ask: You "attended university" in Vienna, where you also learned a thing or two about how to slice a living man's skin from his musculature with a grapefruit spoon, and boy oh boy, don't you wish people would stop watching you eat your vichyssoise.

Whoa, sorry about that, but it does remind us that it's impolite to stare, even at people who eat funny.

Speaking of Europeans, and most of the non-American world: The fork stays in the left hand at all times, and the knife in the right.

The above is known as the Continental style of eating, and it is more logical and efficient than the American style, in which the fork is switched to the right hand for every bite.

Not that you can't eat that way if you want, Cletus.

You order dessert if your host orders dessert.

If you are the host, ask if your guest would like dessert, and act as if you mean it.

To signal to a waiter that you're not finished eating but are merely taking a break for a moment: Place knife and fork as if they are the hands of a clock and it is 4:40.

To signal to a waiter that you're done with a course: Place knife and fork on the plate, parallel to one another, as if it is 4:20.

Warning: These signals won't work at TGI Friday's.

Check-grabbing is just as unattractive in a business context as in a personal one.

Worse: intentionally slow, faux check-grabbing, just in time to fail to attain it.

A pair of suggestions that should take care of this check business: a) You're picking up the check? Oh, thank you; b) Here, let me get this.

If your companion gets the check, you dip into your pocket for the coat-check person.

The Hollywood three-way: You have a business lunch, you split the check, you seek your company's reimbursement for the entire bill, then you write it off on your personal income tax return.

You might want to avoid suggesting the Hollywood three-way at certain sensitive business lunches, such as those at which your future employment is under discussion, or when you're dining with clergy.

Or with your in-laws.

Guidelines for a business dinner: Apply the guidelines for a business lunch, only, you know, later in the day.

Also: At dinner, you might allow yourself that second glass of vino.

We said second, not twelfth.

ask Mr. Etiquette Man!

Question: What are the rules of proposing a toast?

Answer: An important and delicate art, that of the toast-master, and one that can immeasurably enhance an event—and your reputation. A few notes: The host of the affair is the first to make any toasts, which are generally directed to the guest of honor. (If you are not the host, you must seek permission before clanging your spoon against your glass. Also, be very careful clanging glassware—if you break it and soak the table, you'll receive more attention than you wanted.) Toasts may occur at the beginning, midpoint, or end of a meal. At a stand-up reception, aim for the middle of the event, when the most people are likely to be present. First, see to it that nobody's glass is empty, whether they're drinking wine, water, or Cherry Coke. Be sure that you are not drunk. Request everyone's attention (if it's more than a dozen or so people, do so in a standing position), and present your remarks within five minutes, preferably within one. Upon completion, make eye contact with the honoree, raise your glass, and say, "To Bob." If you are on the receiving end of a toast, you don't sip your drink with the rest of the table; you sit there with your hands in your lap. Afterwards, you offer a return toast—a very, very brief one—thanking the host for the hospitality. *Skol. Slainte. Salud.* Cheers.

Chapter twelve

The two o'clock meeting (ha—made you yawn)

In addition to having a prearranged starting time, meetings should have a prearranged ending time.

The two o'clock meeting should never have been scheduled for two o'clock, because everybody will be sleepy after all that vichyssoise.

Unless you believe there's a scarcity in the number of people who hate you, do not schedule meetings cruelly, such as the Friday afternoon of a holiday weekend.

Schedule meetings in the morning, but not too early, and as far in advance as is feasible.

The boss gets the comfy chair at the end of the table farthest from the door.

In fact, the boss *always* gets the most comfortable chair.

Because she's the boss.

Because she's the big-man alpha-dog 800-pound kahuna-huna hooey.

Because of—you guessed it—those gosh-darn boogly-boogly pants!

Of course we have not been drinking. Why do you ask?

Wait until you are instructed to sit, because the boss may have designs on the seating arrangements.

You know that joke, where the junior manager facetiously says, "I suppose you're all wondering why I've gathered you here today"? That's been done.

Meetings should begin even when some invitees are late—it will then be their responsibility to get caught up on what they missed.

It is generally inappropriate for the boss to publicly humiliate people by calling attention to them when they're late to a meeting.

Whether you're running the meeting or merely participating in it, it should be everybody's Job One to a) stay on the subject and b) keep it moving.

What this means: Do not use a staff meeting to push your own parochial agenda.

Way to keep a meeting moving: Confine your input to issues that truly relate to everyone at the table, and reserve more special-interest issues for small-group discussion.

Another way: Offer to put your ideas on paper and circulate them later.

Yet another: Suggest that other meeting participants put their ideas on paper and circulate them later.

Re the previous item: This technique cannot be used on your boss, no matter how egregiously she may be blathering.

Correct! Once again you must defer to those boogly-boogly pants.

It helps, of course, to remember that it is never worse to be late for work than on the day of the morning meeting, when your embarrassment is magnified and publicly displayed for the schadenfreude of all your enemies.

Schadenfreude: The word coined by the Germans for taking pleasure in the misfortunes of other people.

Don't throw around foreign words assuming that others will understand them.

Plus, don't go feeling schadenfreude, anyway, because the world is a fair and just place where either karma or dogma or the afterlife will see to it that eventually everybody gets what's coming to them.

Yeah, right.

Feel free to gloat; just do so quietly and to yourself.

And when in Frankfurt for meetings, don't persist in bringing up that World War II business.

On meetings: It is important that you demonstrate your value by contributing to the discussion.

Your contribution does not start with putting your foot on the conference table.

If you happen to be the boss: You know, of course, to invite to meetings only those people who truly need to be there.

On meetings: Circulate an agenda in advance.

Regarding that agenda: Stick to it.

You know that prearranged ending time for the meeting? That is when the meeting should end.

Regarding meetings at other companies' offices: You don't sit down until someone tells you where to sit down.

And when you're told where to sit, you sit there, feet on the floor (not on the table), arms comfortably in front of you (not laced behind your neck), and your head comfortably erect on your shoulders (not supine on your notebook), no matter how tired or comfortable or madcap you want to be.

At meeting's end, it is also helpful to recap the decisions made at the meeting, so everyone has appropriate marching orders.

What happens at the convention stays at the convention, particularly when what happens has something to do with your boss's inappropriate behavior.

Because she's the boss.

Because she's the big-man alpha-dog 800-pound kahuna-huna hooey.

Because she wears those famous pants.

Speaking of out-of-town behavior, despite the fact that the hotel bill does not explicitly state whether your pay-per-view selections featured pornography, nobody back at the office is going to think you watched *Chicken Run*.

Chapter thirteen

Courtesies and niceties inside and outside the office, including door holding and what to do about people who don't smell right

Regarding holding doors open for women: Forget any admonitions to the contrary and just do it.

Because women love it.

Because men love doing it.

Here's the thing: When the circumstance warrants, you also hold doors open for men.

When the circumstance warrants: when you have reached a doorway first and someone is close behind.

Because door holding is no longer about gender niceties—it's about courtesy and deference regardless of who's carrying the Y chromosome.

141

Because in these times of scarcity, chivalry-wise, such a glimmer of civility and kindness and class brings forth wellsprings of appreciation from either sex—and your actions will be remembered by all who witness.

If a woman should, say, sneer at you for performing such a kindly gesture, feel sorry for her.

Also hold doors for visiting dignitaries and superior officers in your organization, allowing them to precede you.

Similarly, opening the passenger-side car door for your guests before getting into the car yourself is a pleasant and courtly gesture.

You know, come to think of it, your wife might appreciate it, too. And you know, the longer you've been married, the more she'll appreciate it.

It's called respect.

The concept of door holding extends also to elevators, particularly when some poor soul is dashing madly to make it onto yours.

Here's a good one: You stand in the elevator and smile blankly at the person rushing toward you, feinting at pushing the "close" button to tease them.

Okay, it's not *that* good.

The person closest to the exit of the elevator is the first to exit, regardless of gender—a policy best observed in other tight spaces, too, such as tight crevices in caves and narrow tunnels beneath foreign embassies.

If a man and a woman are alone in an elevator, no harm should come to the man who, with a subtle, elegant gesture, invites the woman to exit first.

When holding doors for people, do not do so with a showy, exaggerated flourish. Do not, for example, doff your hat and bow. Just do it in a matter-of-fact way, without calling excessive attention to yourself or your kindly actions.

Speaking of which, as a general principle, there is never a need to doff your hat and bow.

Times not to hold doors open for people: when you're part of a large crowd of strangers surging into a public building, a train depot, say, in which case it shall be first-come, first-through.

One need not carry chivalry to such an extreme as to toss one's coat onto a puddle to protect a lady's shoes—madness, that.

But it is nice to rise from your seat when she arrives at or leaves a table.

You can do this for men, too—not when they effect a temporary exit, to the loo, say, but when they're departing the premises.

Sure, it's a little bit of work, but do it and do so effortlessly and you'll think you're in one of those romantic comedies from the thirties and forties, which, as guides for behavior, rank far above, say, *Porky's.*

No longer necessary and a bit excessive: lighting a woman's every cigarette, particularly since nobody smokes anymore.

What to do when you notice that someone's trousers are unzipped: You affect a Boston accent and loudly hiss, "The bahn door is open at McGillicuddy's fahm!"

That was a joke—particularly the Boston part—and one that even we, its authors, don't fully understand.

You tell this someone quietly and matter-of-factly, "Someone, it looks as if your pants have come unzipped."

Why you do this: because you, too, may someday notice at 5:00 P.M. that McGillicuddy's got a situation down there and that you wore the pink satin boxers and that this unhappy condition has probably existed for hours and hours, including straight through that meeting with the Dutch financiers, seeing as how you haven't used the can since 9:30, and because if a friend had just noticed and spoken up, all this misery could have been prevented.

What you do when you notice that someone has bits of food stuck between his teeth: Presuming he's someone you like and for whom you have esteem, you pull him aside and tell him, "Marty, you might want to check the mirror, because I think there's something stuck in your teeth."

When it's not someone for whom you have esteem:
Indulge in a moment of schadenfreude, chuckling softly to
yourself.

Trickier still—what to do when a coworker has overwhelming body odor: "Cooper, this is rather awkward, but I hope you'd do the same for me. You might want to try a stronger antiperspirant, maybe one of those new brands designed for active people like yourself."

What to do then: Duck.

Bad breath: "Please don't be embarrassed, Alan, this happens to everybody. But since we have the big meeting today, I thought you'd want to know that you've got a slight case of garlic breath."

Other offenses to be aware of: dandruff, greasy hair, flatulence, talking too much, interrupting, failure to wash hands in bathrooms, not covering one's mouth when coughing, and overly luxurious ear and nose hair.

> These news flashes can also be passed along via anonymous notes, allowing all parties concerned to save face.

When someone pays you a compliment, what you say is this: Thank you.

> Arguing with someone who is trying to pay you a compliment will only serve to make you both uncomfortable.

If you feel uncomfortable receiving praise, say, Thank you, something about how it was a team effort, and quickly divert the conversation back to the compliment giver: "Well, thanks, Bob, but you're the one who shoots five hundred yards off the tee, and by the way, great dickie!"

This display of easy modesty has the curious effect of reiterating the greatness for which you just were praised; it suggests that compliments are something to which you are very accustomed, and that, by the act of *choosing* to share credit, you are a leader.

Which reminds us: Do not accept credit for other people's brilliant ideas.

Be too busy to take credit for other people's ideas: Take initiative, be a self-starter, think about future projects.

When speaking about these projects and other projects, speak in terms of "we" rather than "I," to keep the focus on the company as a cohesive group with common goals.

When you have screwed up, do not attempt to pass the buck.

When you have screwed up, take responsibility.

When you have screwed up, your boss usually knows you have screwed up. It only causes harm to attempt to spread the blame to others, making you look like a person of no character.

When you have screwed up, say things like "I made a mistake." Then don't screw up again.

In response to a question from a higher-up, never say, "I don't know." Say, "I'll find out for you."

Brownnosing: Inappropriately attempting to curry favor with superiors by sucking up in a sycophantic, groveling fashion.

Anybody who's seen a movie or situation comedy set in a workplace knows that brownnosers always get it in the end.

ask Mr. Etiquette Man!

Question: How is it that sycophants came to be known as toadies?

Answer: As early as the 1600's, quacks who traveled the countryside selling phony home remedies would employ an assistant to swallow a toad (widely believed poisonous) so that the quack could subsequently "revive" him with his concoctions. This person, who clearly was willing to go to great lengths to please his master, was called a toadeater.

Question: And the origin of the word "brownnosing"?

Answer: If you don't know, you're sure not going to find out here.

Chapter fourteen

I did not have relations with that woman

At one time, low-level managers frustrated by dead-end jobs used to hang in their cubicles a fake sign that read, SEXUAL HARASSMENT WILL NOT BE TOLERATED—HOWEVER, IT WILL BE GRADED, a "joke" that was not funny then and is really, really not funny now.

Just in case somebody missed the memo: Sexual harassment is decidedly real.

Sexual harassment is cruel and devastating and wrong.

We mean to say that sexual harassment is serious business, and that everybody—meaning you— should regard it as such.

Fortunately, it is extraordinarily easy to avoid perpetrating sexual harassment by acting like a decent human being with just the tiniest modicum of professionalism.

Dirty jokes = sexual harassment.

Discussing someone's breasts = sexual harassment.

Repeatedly asking out someone who is not interested= sexual harassment.

Sexual harassment can involve any combination of genders.

You don't need to be the object of someone's sexual advances to be considered a victim of sexual harassment under the law.

Example: "Hostile environment" suits, in which the case is made that management ignores or permits or even condones sexually inappropriate behavior in the workplace.

Example: A person who is offended by your use of that profane word that starts with *f* can report your usage of same to the human-resources department, which is then obliged to issue a formal reprimand.

Then again, scatological words beginning in *s* do not set off those alarms.

Record judgment in the U.S. legal system in a case of sexual harassment: $34 million.

Any questions?

Moving right along. . .

Profanity: no.

The previous is true even if your boss curses
like a stevedore.

Cursing like a stevedore doesn't make you seem like
one of the guys—it makes you seem like a stevedore.

No, we don't know what a stevedore is.

Also: Sobbing at work is to be avoided, as is singing.

It seems obvious, yet it must be said: zero racial epithets, zero ethnic insults, zero gay bashing, zero gender bashing.

These rules do not constitute so-called political correctness. The term political correctness refers to rules imposed for phony, insincere, and intellectually invalid reasons stemming from fashion or politics.

Racial-, ethnic-, sexuality-, and gender-based commentary should be avoided for valid reasons, namely because it demonstrates an unfair and unwarranted lack of respect for whole groups of people.

159

Racial-, ethnic-, sexuality-, and gender-based commentary also should be avoided because it can foster an environment that the groups in question consider hostile in the legal sense of the word, which can make for exciting litigation.

The previous rules apply equally to the most senior executives—such talk in the boardroom will eventually filter down to the mail room, and the mail room is the womb in which the seed of legal action finds purchase.

Again, it should be obvious, but we've all seen this maxim violated: Rules about racial-, ethnic-, sexuality-, and gender-based remarks go double in the presence of clients—especially new or prospective ones.

If for no other reason than you never know which client's mother is Polish or whose uncle is a cross-dresser or whose husband is an Evangelical Christian.

It goes triple where written communication such as e-mail is concerned—e-mail being traceable, storable, and reproducible.

For some of the above reasons, and also because only certain people possess the requisite talent to actually be funny, jokes are best avoided.

Regarding e-mail: Think, just for a moment, of the simple sequence of events that would cause that mash note you composed to Bootyquake5733 to instead go to your CEO.

Or to your wife.

With most e-mail programs, that sequence of events doesn't even amount to a sequence—it involves one errant keystroke.

A similar keystroke could see your proposal for a night of carnality in bunny suits carbon-copied to every employee of your company.

And those mistakes occur not just when you're talking about naughty things. You might be, say, ratting on a colleague or bragging about your job interview at a competing firm or trashing the boss or sending state secrets to Beijing—any of which in the wrong hands could take some burnish off your career.

For that and countless other legal reasons, it's best not to use e-mail for anything other than innocuous, straightforward exchanges of information: ordering staples, scheduling meetings, that sort of thing.

Most companies monitor, at least to some extent, the e-mail of their employees.

In case you haven't gotten the point yet: It might be smart "netiquette" to issue a personal blanket ban on workplace expressions regarding desires that emanate from below the beltway.

That's correct: no porn on the clock.

Mr. Etiquette Man!

Question: When will e-mail suffice for a thank-you note?

Answer: Not often. Mainly when you're thanking a very close friend to whom a handwritten note might seem overly formal.

Question: Is it appropriate to describe such issues as "netiquette"?

Answer: Do we refer to telephone etiquette as "phonetiquette"? To appropriate behavior on submarines as "submarinetiquette?" No. We do not.

No "spam."

No forwarding of lists or jokes or surveys or chain letters or "funny" pictures or "drawings" made with punctuation marks or executable files or anything remotely similar to the aforementioned.

Worse: sending such unsolicited material as attached files, which are in fact documents or programs that require recipients to take the extra step of downloading and opening with the proper software—and thus are even more annoying.

The message you send when you send such things: that you are a complete ass.

Also: that you've spent the last hour or two looking at joke Web sites, which is to say, that you have too much time on your hands.

Put another way: Think of the number of CEOs and Nobel laureates and rising star executives from whom you have received e-mails containing lists of jokes.

Yes, exactly our point.

Chapter fifteen

The four P.M. sales call, wherein Mr. Jones wishes you to contemplate the merits of his company's very special manila clasp envelopes

People who show up without appointments shall be grateful to receive an audience at all and shall not complain if a bit of waiting is involved.

Never show up without an appointment.

Never be one of those people who always make people wait whether they're truly busy or not—and you know you're out there, you nasty, nasty people.

When a person *with* an appointment must be kept waiting more than a few minutes—especially if that person is more important than you are—step out to greet her, apologize, and offer an estimate of when you'll be ready for her.

When you are ready: Apologize again and pay close attention.

You are familiar with the expression "Hold my calls"? Utilize it.

When anyone of higher rank or age enters your office, regardless of gender, you stand to greet them.

You stand to greet entering clients in particular.

You need not stand to receive colleagues of your own rank, your assistant, or other support staff when they approach your desk.

When calling on others: If you've been kept cooling your heels for twenty minutes, you may then ask the receptionist when she expects your host to be available.

When calling on a client: Don't sit on a secretary's desk.

In fact, don't sit on a secretary's anything.

When calling on others: An excellent opening salvo is, "Thank you for your time."

How to get someone out of your office: Glance at your watch and react with genuine alarm, exclaiming something along the lines of "Great horny toads—sorry to interrupt you, but I was supposed to be in a budget meeting ten minutes ago!"

And then: Thank your guest for her efforts and tell her you'll be in touch.

Wriggling out of a meeting: All assistants should be instructed in the use of an escape word, which, when uttered by the boss, brings them running to advise of an impending urgent appointment elsewhere.

Wriggling out of a meeting: Alternatively, the assistant can be instructed in advance to rescue the executive from a meeting at a prearranged time, generally with a phone call apprising her of some kind of emergency.

Better than an escape word: You know you're important when you have an emergency button under your desk.

Chapter sixteen

Afternoon delight: sex in the workplace

Desktop sex is a common fantasy.

The reason desktop sex is a common fantasy is its riskiness, the idea of which many people find exciting.

The aforementioned excitement quickly wilts when the boss snaps on those cold, harsh fluorescent lights—especially if you're on *her* desk.

As with most fantasies, the desktop-sex fantasy is best *kept* a fantasy—or realized atop the privacy of a desk *at home.*

There is no kind of sexual interaction with coworkers or clients that will help your career in the long run.

Cases in point: Donna Rice, Jessica Hahn, Gennifer Flowers, Barney Frank's congressional page.

Yes, those Lewinsky handbags seem to be selling pretty well, but still.

Because the demands of business and the demands of pleasure quite often conflict—almost always, in fact—and when demands aren't met, the demanders can become disappointed.

Which is to say, as a general principle, sex with coworkers or clients is to be avoided.

It is also true that Americans spend a large part of their waking lives at work, and that, as such, relationships with coworkers and clients are hard to avoid.

Which means, when it comes to the office affair, you need to compartmentalize.

Try to keep it secret.

You will fail, but nonetheless, try.

One helpful technique: no public displays of affection.

Public displays of affection shall include, but not be limited to, eye batting, hand-holding, foot massaging, back rubbing, and armpit sniffing.

Point of order: Compartmentalizing one's office love affair does not mean a toss in the broom closet as opposed to a toss on the conference-room table.

Also: There are security cameras in the elevator, and we say that not as a matter of encouragement.

The office affair involving one or more married partners: Break it off immediately.

Exception to the former rule: If the affair is happening between you and your boss, find another job first, then break off the affair.

And remember, here, more than anywhere, the idea of respect, both for your paramour and your coworkers, is of primacy.

Right behind staying employed.

When possible, imbuing the company party with a hoedown theme shall be avoided.

How far in advance to mail invitations to an event: Cocktail party—three weeks. Dinner party, lunch or breakfast meeting—four to six weeks. Day-long conference requiring travel from other cities—up to six months.

The boss must attend the office party, even though she'd rather not, and she must stay for a substantial period of time.

The employees must not exploit their access to the boss at a company party to sell her on their agenda or to ask for more money.

The employees must not exploit their access to the boss to inquire why she was so cheap as to hire only five belly dancers for such a big room.

How to safely juggle a plate of food and a drink at a cocktail party while also greeting people: Grow a third arm or get one of those cupholders that clamp onto the edge of your plate—yeah, that will look impressive—or get the nibbling over with quickly and carry only a drink.

How to avoid becoming overserved at a cocktail party: Don't drink a lot.

Strategy for not drinking a lot: Order a soda with lime and carry it until the ice melts. Repeat.

You were thinking, perhaps that this was just the time to get sauced on the company's nickel and confess your true feelings for Sherm the coffee-cart boy? Wrong.

Seriously: The arrangers of the company party must endeavor to help attendees avoid overindulgence by offering lots of food and nonalcoholic drinks and by limiting the party's length.

The arrangers also should provide for the availability of taxis.

What to do when someone who does not drink alcohol asks for a nonalcoholic drink: Supply such drink without a moment's hesitation and, most important, without any wisecracks.

It is better to provide too much food and drink than to run out of either.

This is the way it works if you're hosting clients, too.

Speaking of clients, if you've done the inviting, you do the looking after.

One does not invite clients to a strip club—at least not on company time or dime.

Even if the client wants to go.

Because her husband might be walking by when you go in.

Now, back to the looking after. The looking after includes paying for all her needs if the entertainment is out of the office, at a bar, a theater, or a sporting event, for example.

If you're the guest, it doesn't hurt to say, "Here, let me get this," the next time the peanut vendor comes round at the ball game.

If you're part of the ball game or golf game, say, there are certain virtues in sportsmanship.

Which means, no showboating, no bragging, no arguing over calls or rules.

Even if you're right.

And here's an idea for when you're playing golf with a prospective client: You let him win is what you do.

Because pride goeth before a sale.

When you are the guest, as opposed to the host, a thank-you note is mandatory.

Chapter seventeen

You don't bring me flowers, although you now and again come through with a Maglite

When selecting a business gift, it's wise to think about the recipient's interests.

The opera tickets to the music buff, for example, and the Jets tickets to the jock.

Verify with other staffers that the gift you've picked is appropriate.

Better yet: Use the corporate-gift specialists on staff at most large department stores.

The corporate-gift consultant not only knows what types of gifts are most appropriate but usually can get you a corporate discount.

Everybody, male and female, likes to get flowers.

Everybody, male and female, enjoys the gift of lingerie.

Oh, behave!

For your assistant: a small, impersonal holiday gift is appropriate, for example, a small gift certificate to a department store.

An assistant who has served you loyally for a decade deserves a gift closer to the $100 area.

The supervisor does not expect to receive a gift from a subordinate.

Wine and spirits have long been traditional business gifts—just aim for a beverage that you know the recipient enjoys.

Before giving wine or spirits to a dot-com e-hole—and there's still a few of them around—make sure he is old enough to drink.

Chapter eighteen

On firing the scalawag you just caught having afternoon delight. On your desk. Plus: dignity when it's your own head on the veritable chopping block

You can't just summon a miscreant to your office and sack him—you must prepare.

Why you must prepare: because the people who decide wrongful-termination suits are the members of juries, and there's a better-than-average chance that people on juries are unemployed or have recently been fired themselves.

Also, if the subject in question is in the middle of a big project, make sure he has finished it and turned it in before you drop the sword, or else you'll never see the goods.

The preparation, which should be a pro-forma procedure firmly in place at your company: Procure his last check from personnel so that after he is axed, he can walk out the door immediately, never to return.

Procure also his reimbursement for unused vacation days, health-insurance information, and data on procedures for rolling over his 401(k), where applicable.

For legal purposes, establish that personnel is satisfied with your documentation of the miscreant's shortcomings.

Rather than thinking of this as personal revenge for someone's lousy performance on your watch—even if that's how you feel—try to take on an air of sympathy, compassion, and support before you cut the guy's legs out from under him.

Re the previous rule: It could prevent somebody from lunging across your desk.

It also can help the newly unemployed in the room save a little bit of face and dignity.

Don't get emotional—remember, this is business.

Remembering that this is strictly business helps one to forget about how you've just made it impossible for the poor sod to feed his three kids, pay his mortgage, and keep up with his wife's exorbitant iron-lung payments.

Also, where appropriate, have a security guard or a hefty, loyal employee nearby.

Make sure nobody in the office can hear you drop the bomb.

Good bomb-dropping language: "I think we both know this isn't working out."

Better bomb-dropping language, considering the possibility that only *one* of you realizes things aren't working out: "This is not working out."

The idea is to not allow for discussion or argument, which can only prolong an uncomfortable situation.

Naturally, you collect all ID cards and keys from the individual, and you do not let him use his computer while cleaning out his desk—he can do major damage.

> The most important advice on firing: Have someone else do it. It is an awful, nasty business, and unless you are a sadist, as one of this book's authors is, it is likely to be the worst thing that you have to do as a manager.

You can't fire me—I quit. Oh? you can? Right, then. I'll just pack up my Maglite and be on my way

Everybody should quit a job in righteous indignation at least once.

How this is done: Step One, climb atop the boss's desk, lower trousers, and…

Now the proper way to quit: quietly, without smashing anything, without cursing at anyone, and with all the damaging documentation you need already carefully photocopied and stored in your home safe.

In truth, you should always produce the most upbeat letter of resignation possible—you never know when you're going to work with these people again.

If you're resigning in protest, briefly and calmly outline your reasons, then include some positive words for the company and your coworkers and close by wishing them well.

Everyone should be fired at least once.

Better that it's not you.

Should it be you, believe it or not, there are certain ways to behave.

If you are laid off as a cost-cutting measure, remain civil.

You might even write a letter thanking your supervisor for all you learned in her employ.

Because when times get better—and they usually do—you may be among the first people she calls.

So *then* you can tell her to get bent.

Which, of course, is a joke.

Because it runs counter to that oft repeated underlying principle of etiquette: Yes, the thing about respect.

Which means you treat people as you would like to be treated by them.

Which means instead of insisting that they engage in some sort of physical reworking of their anatomy, you smile.

You say, Thank you, but no thank you.

And you end it the way it all began: with a handshake.

A handshake that is, we should remind, firm, fast, and free of excess perspiration.

In fact, now that you know the things a man should know about etiquette, there should be very little perspiration at all.